WATER MEMORY

BOOKS BY ROO BORSON

Landfall 1977
In the Smoky Light of the Fields 1980
Rain 1980
A Sad Device 1981
The Whole Night, Coming Home 1984
The Transparence of November/Snow (with Kim Maltman) 1985
Intent, or The Weight of the World 1989
Night Walk: Selected Poems 1994
Water Memory 1996

WATER MEMORY

Roo Borson

M&S

Canadian Cataloguing in Publication Data

Borson, Roo, 1952–
Water memory

Poems.
ISBN 0-7710-1589-5

I. Title.

PS8553.O736W3 1996 C811'.54 C95-932950-1
PR9199.3.B67W3 1996

The publisher acknowledges the support of the Canada Council and the Ontario Arts Council for their publishing program.

Typesetting by M&S, Toronto
Printed and bound in Canada on acid-free paper

McClelland & Stewart Inc.
The Canadian Publishers
481 University Avenue
Toronto, Ontario
M5G 2E9

1 2 3 4 5 00 99 98 97 96

For Kim

Contents

Cloud Music

Hello little buntings, if that's what you are –
you look as though you should be reading the stock
    reports,
keeping up your options on soybeans, gold, and millet.
I married a man once who said the strangest things.
Years later at an airport he knelt down to pray
and the *Playboy* magazines spilled out of his briefcase.
How is it people can go on to become anything at all?
The incomprehensible crystals in the government vault
by which we measure space and time.
The body is impossible. You can hack off every limb
and still it goes on thinking it's whole. It dies,
only to feel it's walking around fully dressed.
Are you in the forest?
One day the grass turns green, and all
the merry little bands of boys
call out to one another in the high, gruff,
sulky voices of robber kings. And no wonder.
This world is only a template for the world,
all painted with a whitewash called Summer Cloud.

Others have been here before you. This cave is older than human thought. All conundra pre-exist, resolvable only by awe. Awe comes afterwards. Colourless, infinitely faceted, more mesmerizing than amethyst, incalculably more valuable than diamond – for these walls and chambers can never be mined, though the imitations are endless. Platoons of students are marched through, they adhere to schedules, they ascend to the outer world, Hong Kong or Toronto, to produce clocks, cookbooks, taxes, with only the vaguest of remembrances. And in *that* world the gorgeous red lips of Margaret McClintock, speaking truth, are like those of the oracles: they say that mathematics is divine. Those two boys who discovered the caves at Les Eyzies, with their hundred-foot dangling oak roots, their pictographs, their ancient riverbed of the bygone race we call our own could not have been more surprised than we. And when she turns and walks away in her black dress and stiletto heels it's as though, for a moment, the whole race stands watching. Watching, mourning the lips of Margaret McClintock, on whose finger rests, light as a bird, the root of two, singing again in the soul of Euclid.

EVERYONE DIES

Everyone dies, yes.
But if Larry dies,
then it is certain.

If Bill Begg ever quits chasing that naked
woman down Spadina in his mind,
if Bill Begg ever really retires,

then everyone must.
Larry hardly did a lick of work
but he never sulked.

They gave Ben Gibson his golf clubs and he died.
They bought Tom Armstrong a watch and he moved to
    Fredericton.
Our Henry got a fishing rod, and I hope

if ever God looks down
He finds Henry happy in Haliburton,
Henry with his cut-outs of Bathing Beauties in a secret
    place,

Henry with his calendar,
every livelong workday X'd
with a big black X.

If where you work is like a family.
If a fourteen-storey building is your home.
If the night cleaner sets down her bucket in the hall

to tell you her left bosom is leaking green pus,
and Bob Carter says you remind him of his daughter,
and if Jack can keep running the marathon, wiry as a fly.

If any of us had a silver dollar.
If Bob Carter would just stay at his lathe.
If Bill could go on daydreaming forever.
Then we could have the conversation.
If anybody had a silver dollar.
If you could ever really quit the workplace.
If these people were not your family.
If you weren't a sister to anybody.

I'm thinking of the smooth green hills where writing comes from, leaf-tips barely peeking from twig-tips, cat's-eye green, the air cooly smooth against the cheek as a refrigerated egg.

The new green hills are green, as green as memory, and as old. The house, as usual, a wreck, the first sowbug of spring advancing across the floorboards, beyond control, the millipede that rushes up, all summery, from the bathtub drain. Come Sunday we'll go out for dim sum again, the elderly at rest behind their newspapers, the young in party clothes, the moonwhite noodles thick and fragrant on the plate. That the living can feed on such stuff. Dead matter, dead meat.

If a word is repeated, let it be the contexts that rhyme. Not glibness, that party trick – having to dunk one's head in a martini reciting "Skunk Hour" over and over, till you're sick.

No language now, only the day and circumstance. Not the pedigree of words, what they might be in French, or whether this is of significance.

I'm thinking of the smooth green hills where writing comes from. Two kinds of thinking. What kind of thinking when it rains?

UP

Up and into the world,
into the smell of the mouths of human beings,
into streets, the gale of the subway,
newspapers shuddering, the rattling track
into old Jerusalem, Sumeria, the Eaton Centre,
where the buying and selling begin before dawn
with the bread vendors and coffee merchants.

The day begins with vengeful bells,
an indeterminate number of sandgrains,
the alarm ringing out through the asphalt of the school-
    grounds,
and any one of us must keep on,
polishing our eyeglasses over and over,
and the lightest of ephemeral rains
keeps falling and vanishing.

Up into the world,
where there's never a *Hold it!* or *Wait for me!*
where *Business is business,*
where *The merchant class has grown too strong,*
as has often been remarked.

PRIVATE HAPPINESS

I know I'm happy when I start humming in the morning,
holding my orange juice like the lethal weapon
an Aunt once said it was so I should
walk, not run, upstairs with it, or I'd be sorry.
As for me, I'm happy just to not be living in New York.
Also that I'm standing straighter than before.
The doctor's a flatterer. Examining my spine he said
he figured I was smart enough to get the picture
without pictures of how people'd ended up before –
that is, to do my exercises.
Elsewhere that sort of thing might pass for pleasantry.
Here in Toronto the snow in sulky patches lies,
and soon it will be spring again, as the robins foretell.
Six autumnal pears huddle in a basket won at a party once,
decades ago, a basket funereal and tidy as a Jackie Onassis hat.
The pears summer-sunburned, burnished. I know
the one I'll eat. It points toward me like a fortune cookie.

MY LOVER AND I HAVE A PACT

My lover and I have a pact,
and sometimes we walk in the forest, breath to breath,
among the great cores of being.
We stamp over the wooden footbridge,
we're happy animals,
the nasty little child in us
runs at the ducks, flapping!

Please fall in the icy river, child.

But disaster is everywhere.
One by one, the people we've known.
Bam! Kapow! go the phone calls and letters.
My own brother built rockets beside the basement door.
I'd crouch there with him among the rubber bands and
    matches.
Years later, when I finally stood up,
it was on the mined sands of Gaza. "Don't move!"
they yelled, not daring to come for me –
but I was already long gone,
thinking about the romantic profile of a boy I'd just met.
He was from New York, my own age, and liked driving
    racing cars.

HOME

Those two
colourless
mites I snuffed with my thumb
a moment ago

along the page
(age-spotted, velvet-edged)
of the *Home*
Book of Italian Cooking, running

was it, or for all I know
just taking their time
between Fresh Tomato Sauce and
Plain Tomato Sauce

skirting the crossed
rubber bands that have held
the book together these
thirty-odd years

Mine! Mine! I felt,
and crushed them,
my childhood, what
are you doing
there.

And the limbs become heavy with longing, and the bones, and the eyes half-closing are heavy, and the arms in their light summer clothing. Limp as a sleeping child we are carried upstairs, beyond geography, history, the science of singing, the tickling vibration of it, the "bright" sound when we sing from the resonating cavities inside the head, the "dark" when we sing from the chest . . .

And it climbs the vertical walls of the beaker, year after year, to the astonishment of students, still so childlike in their fears and yearnings – barely, like fawns, beginning to stand on their wobbly capacity for true thought. They never knew! They weren't told of this property of the world, the solid state suddenly liquid, seeping upward like Helium-4 or the weather, climbing the straight-walled vessels of glass and brimming over, heavy, liquid, overflowing every container . . .

Until it forms even from the air, far from the laboratory, coalescing in large drops which splash our clothing and noses with temperate pleasures as we begin to hurry down a corridor of the city, even the most fashionable couples reaching out a hand to run, glazed and spotted, with a giraffe's awkwardness – running now, hand in hand under the canopy of summer storm.

BEET SALAD

I'm baking three beets in the oven
and reading and waiting
for self-revelation. And thinking
of the clayey breast these hearts
were pulled from, three in one,
woody and hard and heavy and ever
more adjectival and smelling of vegetable:
of chopped trunk and cut onion
and severed life, and sweet
as Seder wine or the wine of Christ,
with or without believing. And of my own
breast, after thirty-nine years
of beating and thinking and eating,
of hearts grown woody or leathery . . .

The beets must be baked
an hour or more, depending,
then tested: resistant,
rootish, matured in earth –
you'll like to lick the fork.
Next let them sit.
Pull down a good book while they cool,
then cut them through,
pricked here and there
by the cheap tines of appetite.
Mixed with new yogurt
and masses of fresh dill

the colour is spectacular.
Chill as desired.
Then eat.

And someday I may tell you, if I know,
how I came to these words and this place,
with the house to myself, and sunset,
eating beet salad, flamingo-pink, and reading.

MY LIFE IN AN EIGHTEENTH-CENTURY JAPANESE PRINT

Overindulged
in strudels,
sick,
unfinished with grief,
another infinite afternoon
on Yorkville's streets . . .

Duck then
into the faint sea-smell
and ascetic calm of the print store.
The passionate, bad-breathed owner.
The past.
The prints giving off the rarefied gas
of an extinct code, where,
browsing among oversized binders,
under the artful glare, the living eyes
of the dead masters, I happen upon
myself, but in another life.

Black hair, white breasts, a warrior's nonchalance –
you wouldn't have recognized me!
A strange man,
a paper room,
our sexual organs at the centre,
out of scale, enormously engorged.
Two hundred years! And back then,
to the streets again. Back,
thanking the owner.

But how strange everything is.
Such clear light.

An entire world swept clean of sorrow!

STARTING THE TAPE

for David McFadden

After we'd made it through the aerobics section and the endurance section and the stretches, our teacher reminded us that today was relaxation day, she switched off the lights and we lay down against the pitch-dark of our closed eyes, in free-fall really, but kept afloat in this world by the special exercise floor which had cost the county taxpayers dearly (it was worth it of course, being no mere floor but a raft of salvation) and our teacher started the tape. I heard her lie down too as we breathed out and out and the voice on the tape guided us along, but instead of repeating to myself with each exhalation the intended phrase I could think only *Il Vecchio is our love*, over and over, and it worked as well as anything, I felt my individuality disengage from me, and with it its hobo's sack of joys and troubles, which was no more than an old handkerchief, really, knotted to a stick and presented to me by two long-ago best friends as I set off on my first trip east, and which I still keep, neatly folded in the top drawer, minus the stick. I experienced the tension in the buttocks, thighs, and feet, and then the smoothing out, felt myself tacking toward an approximation of perfection achieved only by ball bearings manufactured in space under near-gravityless conditions, and I sensed the others nearby, their corresponding stillnesses, as we lay randomly aligned along the singular plane of the aerobics floor, as nearly identical as we can be in this life.

Lying there I recalled many things, strands, as it were, of the softly playing music . . . the afternoon a nostalgic chef in Vancouver, exiled from whichever Old Country he had fled, concocted a fruit omelette in honour of our love;

my jewellery box full of irreparable wristwatches; a single moment of inexcusable cruelty on an afternoon years ago, having just finished refilling the cat's food dish. He had been sick of late and, being near to death (although I didn't know it then), continued to stand there, howling mechanically, until, in vexed helplessness, I grasped the back of his head and turned it, saying, uselessly, and lowering myself in my own estimation as I did so, *Look; food; eat.* After a moment's pause he went on as before, weeping at the ceiling, because he had to, his hunger was for no mortal food.

I was breathing in and in now, silently pronouncing *I'm full of energy*, but in a tone of irony the voice on the tape would never condone, when it came to me that a sense of irony is merely the rebellion of the still-young-at-heart, which could only mean that I was more full of energy than I had admitted. After class I went home and continued reading a book of poems called *Gypsy Guitar* until it was time for the news. It seemed the writers' strike had ended, and the poker-faced buffoon whom the news team had rewarded with a short spot on the subject declared, in the end, "Let's face it: we live in a thirty to forty channel world," and for him that seemed to sum it up.

Somebody at the next table was eating oysters, somebody else was eating clams, and George, beside me, whom I'd only just met, said he couldn't bring himself to eat oysters or clams or any other creature whose *whole body* lies in front of you, no matter how small or ugly. I ordered a Caesar salad, and after dinner we all went over to the reading, where George read a wonderful poem about his father and a bowl of tomato soup. When I told him I loved the poem he said everyone has memories of a father eating something, even if not tomato soup: that is, the poem could be lovable only if people made their own substitutions . . . whereupon deep inside me a miniature person stood up and shouted *No!* – not so loud as to disturb anyone, mind you, but *No!* – because love won't abide substitutions, and what the poem made me love was *his* father, not to mention tomato soup. At the reception afterwards, everyone had gotten their drinks and we were standing around eyeing the arrangements of crackers, when George – apparently failing, in the face of the onrushing sentence, to locate the word "crustaceans" – referred to the shrimp (keeled over, peeled and cooked on their little platter) as "Etruscans," and all of us standing around the end table began to laugh, to laugh and eat (except for George, of course) as if in homage to the ancestors, and the agile minds they passed down between us.

MOTEL

No. I won't envy the people who check into a motel
throw their bags down on the bed
and dash off without a thought to the adjoining
    restaurant
because it advertises Dancing Till Midnight –
and they don't even bother to check the menu!
Give me a room with furniture
and I'll go tapping along it, shedding clothes,
I want to know what's real. A television and a bed,
my predecessor's single pubic hair in the tub
like a solitary pearl. If art consists in saying a thing
at the only point in history it *can* be said,
well then the life of art is the only life.
Why envy the other guests their credibility? Or the youth
at the Front Desk. To be young is to be cheerful, cruel,
and reverent; keeping watch at the Front Desk
to be radiant among mercenaries.
No.
If I have to choose a species, give me cats –
skulking along perimeters, astonished
by fluffballs,
table legs,
tiny glasses of Advocaat!

EARLY MUSIC

5:14 in the morning say
before the "rushing to their doom"
of the weekday rush hour
the Q.E.W. the 401
the quiet onramps

how the birds have been at it
for over an hour
lodging complaints airing announcements
shouting out their Christmas lists
in Chinese, Swahili, Arabic –

Sometimes I think
there must be a new kind of god
to whom one might pray
at times like this.

Al Purdy maybe,
in checked pants,
besotted,
wandering the dewy morn
of Ameliasburg.

VOCATION

Night after night on the kibbutz
they berated me for staying out late, watching the moon.
Drink your milk, they said –
in the morning you'll have to work. All day
you'll be picking melons and apricots,
you'll be hungry. Only houseguests and poets
can afford to be as lazy as you!
Night after night they berated me.
And night after night, my cup of milk shining,
I came out to you.
Drink your milk, I said.
In the morning you'll have to work.
All day you'll be picking melons and apricots,
you'll be hungry. Only houseguests and poets
can afford to be as lazy as you.

LYING IN BED READING ROBERT GRAY

Lying in bed. Another day –
                                        another day of waiting
waited for too long
in a life made
short by definition
and now
at a trifle
the long day ruined.
Out the window, *gum trees, his* –
                                        and in the rainy
subtropics of a calm half-claimed by melancholy,
rain on the leaves. Transparent window lizard.

That we make it so
is true;
that we shorten the faulty
daydream of the time ahead with
waiting, disappointment –
                                        but that
doesn't *make* it so.
My transparent friend in the window
moves
with clocklike
spareness, doesn't
think much. Prefers a sort of poetry,
in particular the wind
and leafy wet of his own country. Window.

Window. Gray day, Gray's books beside me,
his house of lizards.
(What do you feed them?
Nothing.)

(How do you live with them?
Side by side.)

SNAKE

"A gardener's snake," the city employee told me,
a snake no bigger than a shoelace
(himself a gardener) – holding it curled
once around the thumb and once
around the fingers of a hand –
a mitten of a snake
on possibly the last day of summer warmth.

The snake was avidly licking at the air,
its tongue like a Tibetan banner
or a young eel
of black silk –

We stood a little uneasily,
on the common path before winter,
the air around us golden,
like a temple wall.

If to record is to love the world,
let this be an entry.

WHUFF

Cousin to the slug, this flesh, fish-bait, excess
I love you with
now that I'm not young or slim or lucky
except in love. If luck it is
to lie beside you, sleepless,
hour on hour, moonlight in the room –
not knowledge or luck or love
but breathable stone. And you do,
you breathe it in. You *whuff*, you snort –
and all the pebbles, all the sands
are raked against my eardrums . . .
this your nightly catechism, only catechism,
that I know you'll never learn,
charmed, asleep, yourself –
as I am young again beside you,
and flesh, and wakeful.

THAW SONG

Mouths of water
eyes of the eastern rain

hold me, will you
or else
erase this.

Fly out
fly out from the hive of summer –
glitter like snow

all those years of abandon ago.

Title and Subject

Water does not remember, it moves
among reeds, nudges the little boat
(a little), effloresces a shadowy fog
which forgets for us the way home
though the warm dry rooms are
in us. (Stretched on the examining table we
feel it when the unfamiliar hand
presses just there.) Water,
on its own, would not remember,
but herd follows herd, and memory is a shepherd
of the gentlest wants. Not even blood
can recall, though the live
kidney shipped in its special box
wakes up one day in someone new.
No one made this world, there's no need
to feel ashamed. Be water,
find a lower place, go there.

THAT YOU

That you are quick and warm and in the world
though everything is against it –
death, fires, unloveliness –
except my skin,
except my hair.
That you are in the world
– and the plains are mountains
– and a drop of Bloor Street rain
might yet reach the Mediterranean . . .
That you are quick and warm as a living vein,
and it runs beneath the hair, near my mind.
Oh I am in the world too, though I'm lazy.

MOON TUB

Tincture of moonlight the stranger said,
our heads afloat, our bodies
sunk like stone . . . all of us strangers,
looking up together, having forgotten
the formula for finding the North Star,
like so many others, idly, before and after –
whatever our lives might depend on.
We joked around in the warm water, and someone
was offended a little at being wrong. He was the one
who'd said *tincture of moonlight.* My faith
had gone a-maying. I had forgotten even my friends,
so alike, indistinct in their bright blurred cities.

That was two days ago. The gentlemanly figure
waiting on the sill as if for a porter or
an open door has gone. If I didn't
love you I'd become a nun right now,
or a crane-fly. Something other.

EYES

Not what they see, but a green shade
where the forest dozes, bear-flecked,

or we're sailing: blue on blue,
the harbour full of sun –

and afternoons:
what blue is

to brown,
or hazel to hazel, the

company we keep,
mossy or marine –

not the black
hatch to the mind –

but of
more painterly things.

To fall, looking. Sleep,
all the summer days there.

SPRING THINKING

That desire should be embodied
so finely, so finally:
delight, eyebrows,
unkissed yet, or ever –
but petals peeling
in the rain and wind,
plum and cherry bells,
especially
the vertical
pear: quill-like,
preened by bees and sunlitness,
giving way to leaves
and the primacy of summer fruit.
Meanwhile, how we pick our way
through talk,
the latest movies, etc.
The lilac not yet bloomed.
Nor yet
the honey made from lilac.

MARGARET LIVINGSTON

I married Tom Lathrop under the giant sequoia
at John Muir Elementary School in Grade Three.
It was Recess.
We said our vows and the bell rang.

In Grade Four Eric Slattery made eyes at me,
and he didn't stop
till Grade Five and Art Class: Sue Martin.
Her blonde bangs and fresh round-faced loveliness.

I made friends with Sue Martin.
Made friends with Margaret Livingston,
her gold ponytail and yard of yellow roses.
And with dark-eyed Alison.

All winter we'd walk down Russell together, early,
streets named for men and women,
though nothing but the names remain –
and Betsy Partridge could barely finish half an ice cream

before her pale arm would flag. Does the little creek
still run beside the Lunch Room? In its runoff
from the hills the boys would
hunt for frogs and the girls shy like horses.

I remember Sally too, the girl my father
spoke of once, as if immortal –
though now he's in his grave. Sally of the golden curls,
who was before my mother, or me.

BROWNIE

Early in the morning, when the world smelled good
and the crabgrass was still crisp with dew, I'd go and lie
beneath the apple tree. Teacup blossoms on a flat blue
    sky –
and Brownie would be sighing lightly, excited to have
    me near.

Brownie had brown eyes, and a coat as glossy
as a chestnut mare's. A German Shorthair,
trained in dog school, military style. We'd taken him
for the summer, as a favour to a family friend.

For hours he'd cry, penned up alone,
and then we'd bring his food and touch and hug him,
and go away, back to the house,
dawdling through the lengthening days. And Brownie

would wail, then whimper, then whistle in his sleep.
We weren't allowed to let him out or play with him,
that kind of thing would spoil a dog for hunting –
and we ate those ducks each holiday,

peppercorns of tarnished shot
you bite on, like a filling coming loose, coughing out
the soft mouthful of flesh that smells wild
and fresh, of shit and flight and distance.

When summer was over, I went away
sighing from that place, afraid they would shoot him.
A whole summer "going up on the hill" as we called it –
and still do sometimes, seldom and alone,

to think some problem out. A good place
to make good decisions. *If only*
I had stayed with him, I felt –
and after he had gone, I went up there.

I was young, and lost in the infinite, tufted with
    blossoms.
I wanted thinking to take me up.

MILK

When I was young I drank milk by the fire.
It would have been early evening,
and the fire made of appleboughs
from the newly pungent trees.
The pot lid banged onto the pot,
and the house slowly bloomed
with the smell of turnips.

A house is a simple construct.
The builders die, but it goes on.
And still every childhood matters,
like mint grown in the shade,
all translation is painstaking,
and has no natural melody.
The world may be old,
but even then it was old,
without end or beginning.

LIFE AMONG FLOWERS

I would like to lie down on a leaf of banana
under a blue sky on a summer day,
and never die. To live among flowers,
but as a vocation: to press my face
into the velvet face, unimpressed by pain.
Tiny non-violets dwell in the purple pedestal
of the bromeliad, the hornrimmed tortoise
sweeps her winglike legs over moss and swampwater,
our luckless pennies . . .
Sequoiadendron Giganteum, Pendulum,
though you let drop not a syllable
I keep still as a disciple, I'm a northerner
and born to be your slave. Yet we love most
what we've learned to love,
whatever is most strange. Ears and oars of cactus,
their sprays and polka dots of spines,
their blooms like wilted gowns, life candid and
    unastonished,
as we lounge in the tub with our *National Geographic*s
or sit rigid in the waiting room, the open desert
on our laps: the split crimson of the evening fruit,
from which the smiling bat looks up,
his little furred fox-face blooded and content.

In school we were taught to think clearly, or – at the
very least – to print neatly.
We learned to print neatly, with the threat of "at the very
least" hanging over our heads, the way the antlers and
replacement eyes of the motheaten stag hung above
the clock in the auditorium.
In the playground whosoever's stone landed outside the
square or touching a line was "out." Whosoever's
stone landed inside the square was "in," and could
take a turn.
The teacher would wave us as one group across the
playground, then she would wave us back again.
At night it rained.
Those who didn't know the rules refused the rules,
couldn't refuse the rules.
And at night it rained, the rain washed away the world.

Totally dark now over western New York, and darker still
in some other time zone, the radio voice ringing out

and the Niagara River's art deco-esque falls and ineffable
cathedral glow, those magic lightbulbs we had as kids

that gathered light all day, secretly, milkily green
till the sun went down, and then shone in our palms in
bed –

or Ashland
Kentucky from the night interstate, no longer a radiant

vision but the substance of Hell: no heat,
a cool planet never walked on,

Pluto. No telling who we are as we're going there,
depending on the season and the geese, who listen

for diverse engines as a kind of background music
to flight. Happiness

is non-representational, like a Persian border,
or the plate of biscuits and cream gravy

that keeps recurring in the middle of the country, much
as God
appears blazing in domes and crosses in the Middle East,

or as over time menus become iconic, suggestive
of a long decline, though the trip hasn't really started

till we've settled on something: hamburgers one way,
cottage cheese another, with canned peaches. You pick

your favourite and stick to it
until we get there, the high sky of the open country

where all our sickness and depression and belief
vanish, vanishingly high, with all the small clouds
    drifting east.

In the mustard-coloured-raincoat-dappled streets
enormous hot dogs are being bought
and eaten, they softly steam
like spring rain from hard ground.

Which rain is the very first?
And how do we know
every cracked pane will be replaced,
all crookedness be mended now there's time,

so the doors and the gates can stand open and friendly,
and a breeze roll in over the sills
from as far away as we like?
Fish slanting in piles and old ice skates,

both shining.
So many new young mothers turning aside in public
    places,
blouses hiked up
over the huge breast weeping milk.

The housecat treads more heavily because of you.
With a thrump and a thrrrump!
It's true!

You are the amphitheatre,
and with you arrive
wings, leaf-tips, epithelia, song –

You comb the frozen hair of those who sleep in the park.
And count it, frouzle it.
Palpable whim,

you throw a switch –
and hats, gloves, fur-bearing jackets
sit stupefied.

The lies!
Tell us,
do.

With all the dusty road still to go,
and summer a-coming,
and the first ripe strawberries.

TO THE GREY SQUIRREL

O cats of rectitude,
scavengers of the great All,
limb-rats, monkeys
of the northern forests, you
who steal chocolate from my sill
and hunker, impenetrable, on delicate haunches,
to prise it from its wrapper –
what is all my praise of you
compared to a nut?
Startled or restful,
you make no sensible sound,
diminutive, itinerant,
but recede across the vistas of the city park
like a skipped stone.
O mink of the ancients,
arboreal beaver,
parodist of the hunt, your chin
recalls long lines of royalty,
your coat, the royal gown.
And where I for no known reason keep
a houseful of objects,
you, assiduously digging,
make an investment of hunger.
You smite the lawn of my neighbour!
You bury your plunder.

SPAIN

This bed is mine, and everything on it!
Crumbs, cat hairs, the cat Toby
teething on his favourite
Milk Lunch Biscuit – even the clammy
gummed bits. I claim them.
I claim them for Spain.
Also all underwear, tissues, pieces of mail,
the moth that knocks itself
silly against the bulb and falls, folded,
into *Lady In The Lake*, page fifty-seven.
All! All are mine.
Even the sprigs that spring
(such dark, such heathen gold)
from the knuckles of your toes.

You leave the city and I'm free,
i.e. for nothing, to get drunk with friends.
And stumble home late, asking
the Important Questions. Such as:
Why did you go?
What are you that I love you?
What's so important in Poughkeepsie
that it deserves you, even for a night?
Strangeness; loose ends; my body on the far side of
    the bed
desiring me.
Is this how it will be?
If you would help me, John Donne, help me –
prescribe a metaphysic
for when in Rome, Atlantis, all the wronged cities –
and they send for him, and he's gone.

REREADING JAMES MERRILL
(SHERATON EL CONQUISTADOR)

I have overheard them talking
two by two beside the pool:
captains of industry running tabs,
and wives of industry,
and the spectre of their young,
and what they say. And every day at noon
the red-pated woodpecker battering his beak
against the sinuous eucalypt. It merely sways.
Ghosts, words –
but for you I'd be idle and sad.
Late at my coffee. Early to drinks.
Is that lonely or bad?
The women sit waiting for husbands,
or maybe a sign – and evening approaches.
Nobody hears what I think.
The desert is courtly, and pensive. Quail rush
from place to place like queens,
until the golfer's day is done.
And then at dusk the most marvellous rabbits come
to scamper on the greens,
as in a play by Aeschylus.

SLEEP IN THE AFTERNOON

The book of bad translations
has fallen from your hand,

and once more you are called to leave
the heavy body on the bed,
drifting with the syllables *Wang Wei,*
just before rain.

The herds and the riders come galloping,
Mongol and Persian,
drumming their hooves over the roof,
stirring up perfume among the pines –

drifting, then gone.
Field glasses and tympanum,
accidental lilies left behind . . .

Come back! Come back!
Stroke my forehead, rain –

WAKING THE GHOST OF DU FU

Long into the night the frogs carouse,
waking the ghost of Du Fu.
Hush, I say, but then get up,
and pour myself cold tea.

Crazed with hunger my daughter bit me, crying . . .
Pity the critic who would write of such a work.
May he never be granted a position!
Better, let him be lauded
in moderation, then sent across the western desert . . .

Poverty? It's relative. Welcome, brother. Lift up your cup.
Your songs are no longer out of favour.
And all those who would have kept you from life
lived only to die unknown, far from Ch'ang-an.

Continuous Elegy

SHE IS SLEEPING

One I love is sleeping
sleeping

she of the soft knees sleeping
who loved my father
whom my father loved
(though what is true?)

she of the soft knees is sleeping
but did he notice them first
or later
those knees

or was it her proud head
like a horse's
grazing
as she looked upon the world

was it her proud head he loved
with its thin brown mane now silver
and her eyes that dwell upon fields
and ox-eye daisies
and buttercups
and windflowers
(and who among us
will remember the windflowers?)

she who reads the news like everyone else
who looks upon the world
and sees fields
who keeps the names of flowers
and gives birth to me.

TO BE HERE

To be here with a headache is better
than not to be here
with or without one.
Lying in a room with only
one small window
I tell myself this, and it's true.
The weevil burrowing
in the flour sack
is how I am,
how I'd still like to be sometimes,
burrowing my head
into the apron
of the woman who fed and loved me.
I lie quiet
and the clouds pass my window
like puffs of flour. I remember
the white apron,
how my tears and impatience
would disappear there.
I remember her brown arms,
the pie she was making,
the strips of ragged pastry, sugared,
that always came first
straight from the oven.
But the flour of the clouds
is not the flour of the woman
who has gone with her brown arms
into the earth.
I think of her hum when I work now,
and the chords of the sunwarmed river
make me want to lie down still again,

with the birds crossing my narrow window.
They cross it so suddenly,
out of earshot,
piled with clouds.

I'm tired when I think of my mother.
The tiredness is in the stooping,
in the thought of bending
all day over the garden,
and in the lines of spring.

Because it's spring, my father has become
very light in my mind.
The lightness is the lightness of an empty
suitcase you pick up,
thinking that it's full.

Maybe it's this lightness which makes me
tired when I think of my mother, think of her
still mixed with roses,
still with roots,
in the April rain.

The room is a musty Long Island room we arrived in only yesterday, having crept through the eye of the needle which is the Lincoln Tunnel to what we imagine must be the city of self-loathing though it goes also by other names. Scrap of paper improvising a slow poised ballet at the base of a sign saying *The Taxpayers Pay For Littering*, the *The* crossed out and replaced by *Us*, which nobody reads. My father won't be coming back again, nobody does. Eventually his atoms will suffuse the universe – on camelback, police car, fern – travelling to all the places he only read about. Somewhere in the middle of any argument the engine breaks down, no point continuing. The wind and the rain. I sleep beside a fellow for whom sleep and snoring are one: he growls gently like a hunting cat but wakes without remembrance. Nothing to report beyond the rare condition of togetherness, this side-by-sideness, part figment, part fruition. A room in Long Island, the wind and the rain, America, where everyone's on a first-name basis. My father won't be coming back again.

PERSONAL HISTORY

I only saw Warsaw
once, and in a dream, and yet
I'm recognized, just once –
in 1983 – by my cheekbones.
Out of nowhere. In the way a poem
is a poem and part of the truth,
or part of the story.
My father loved history, the way some admire
the permanent movement of rivers
or the migration of basalt –
but he didn't like personal history.
He was born in Columbus Ohio,
and now the grass grows over him,
whom I loved.

HEREDITY

Dog barking down the long
barking street in the dark

the scuttling of
fallen lemons and then

rest dripping eaves relieved
of rain

the chromosomal changing of the guard
in the black muscular cell
of the ant path

blue veins
behind her knees
as she dressed

woe woe
the evening owl

TULIPS

Someone you love dies
and pain shoots up out of the ground.
Yellow & red.

In the small difference daybreak makes,
maybe 3° maybe less,
a tulip might begin to open.

3° is
more than enough
to melt glaciers,
and submerge continents.

Dawn merely touches it
and the snake moves off,
released from its spell.

The sun rises like the
Queen of England's smile,
bestowing condolence
equally, everywhere.

A small promontory
on the tip of Chile.
Rarotonga, to the west.
But sleep:

sleep is arbitrary.

PICNIC FOREST CRATER RHYME

Picnic

We're still afraid of the dark and cold.
But the sun is out. Swans laze on the pond.

A scrap of sandwich wrapping
(*why is it*?) ignites a filament of fear.

All the world
lit with it.

Forest

I've been here before
and I'll come again

if I ever leave. The forest
is homeless. Tree.

Tree.
Nothing lives here.

Isn't it lonely or wrong?
A salamander

pink and strange as a finger
reaches half-luminous under a leaf.

The caterpillar sews itself upside down
to sleep and change,

but I'm the one who sleeps and changes.

Crater

I've lived in this bed a month or so.
News is as far away as sleep is.

If you come to grief
there's nothing to do. You sleep

or might as well.
Afternoon was made for this,

at least it has a use.
Administer news five times a day,

it has a use.
My mind

is craters.
Now and then

someone will
land there.

Rhyme

What is it shivering in the kitchen,
balled up on the floor beside the stove?

Is it a kitten? Is it the cold?
Show me the girl who will never grow old.

DISMEMBERED VILLANELLE

New daylight on the unmade bed.
You have to leave the dead behind.
Nights we make love on the very spot
where someone might have died.
You have to leave the dead, they won't leave you.
You have to leave them as you'd leave a lover
for another lover, or another two.
I pressed her lightly with my fingertip,
as sometimes I press you.
I was a day too late, they'd left her as a strange
reminder not my mother there was
nothing left for me to do.
We took the bed.
We took the bed because I wanted to.
The bed I used to lie in as a child
and sleep between them when I couldn't sleep.
Where I am lying here with you.

I stood beside the dark polished
end table like meat, while they made out
the death certificate, you had to
be there, etc., and I am, my
copper-coloured hair falling over the pages,
deer browse nearby, I'm nearly fourteen
and can never take you there. Instead
let me show you the steps where I prayed, *I am*
NOT a member of the rat race,
over and over, all my working days.
The steak comes up from the landfill unscathed,
we can read the news decades later and
laugh, literally, at our favourite table,
in our favourite piazza,
near the corner where someone waited
a whole year for the light to change, saying
Mama, Mama, under her breath,
and the light of the whole sky
falling on her copper-coloured hair, and the steps
where she prayed, and the
dark polished end table, that was like meat.

DROUGHT

From the floor of the great river
the broken ribcage of a long-lost paddlewheeler
rises in the mud.
Someone holds up a nail.

Day by day, like birds,
one droplet at a time,
we are learning to bathe
in an inch of water

while syrup sweetens in the trees
and wild azaleas
bloom as never before. The river's memory
is soft and deep. I must sit

on the edge of the bed in the dark
and very slowly
sip
from a glass.

I know my true friends by how well
they put up with my whining, which they think of
as a kind of song. That way,
when they think it's been sung long enough
they can tell me very gently to fuck off.

My poor tooth is gone for good! And still
it's right here, half-wrapped in gold
like a chocolate,
at breakfast as in the afterlife,
amid the sunshine and cereal and daffodils.
What would my mother say, who once paid a man

to fix my teeth so I'd be beautiful, and have a happy life?
All I could do was ask for it back,
remembering the pickled herring jar
of molars in the bureau drawer,
and the family gall stones
mysterious as myrrh.

I'm missing a tooth, but what really worries me
is that I don't have a mother anymore,
someone to turn to, open wide, and say *See?*
And then for her to smile, and smooth my hair,
the one who made me.

IT'S RAINING

A rich rain is falling and my mother is nowhere to
hear it.
Bells, bells, bells –
thunder's huge omniscient wheels passing over us.
But we with our thoughts are
not crushed, surely.
Only the dog is,
ears flat,
shivering where he lies.

LATE LUNCHEON

Mozart, Mozart, what a fate!
To be piped in softly,
over the centuries,
to the horsing-around of the
kitchen help before closing.

I came here in despair,
eating butter like a food.
How glad I am of your music!
That it can be
both blind and deaf . . .

and such a voice
should sing to you in the grave,
coming always with news,
to sate the undying curiosity of the dead . . .

Instead you sing to me, over my soup.

Such a roomful of tables though,
already set for tomorrow!

Except one, just there near the pillar –
I suppose they haven't noticed.
Only a napkin and a knife
for each place,
and two rolls like smooth stones
on the little plates.

Such patience across the empty table!

RAINY DAY LETTER

for Jan Zwicky & Don McKay

Pine. Pine dust. Detritus. And now
a seat at the foot
of doubtful shelter
for the rain's recital of Chopin
cum Tatum cum assorted
symphonic thoughts and discards
à la Mozart.

Cold, rain, exile from friends. Happiness
is a stone beside my foot. I could pick it up
if I wanted to. Pick it up
and put it down, thinking of you.
A warm kitchen somewhere.
Downpour.
Then it's over. Take a breath
and jog down the path
strewn with sunwet, lesser rocks,
beneath dripping pine vaults,
dull jewels of insular purpose.
Pale pagodas and penises still risen
from the forest's previous night's wet dream.
Odd fancies live in us too,
popping up from buried mycelia.

Last night's lightning hit close,
and just for a second
the lights went, and the computer,
banishing this half-finished letter.

BELOVED

1.
A few orangey streetlamps, and the sky yet light with a blue light: twigs and hanging pods, their darkened curves there. By the window, waiting for whoever it is you love. The swish of a distant car, and then another, every sound that passes bound for home. Something savoury simmers on the stove. It's October. You kneel in the warm narrow circle of a lamp, keeping watch for the beloved.

2.
On stepping through the door we smell this smell:

stray hairs. Skin flakes. Chairbacks dulled by sweat.
Pillows,
the phone book,
wooden spoon handles darkened by our touch.

3.
In all of the places I become lost. In cafes, markets, movie lineups. In every place you are lost to me. Then, above the heads in the department store, across the packed restaurant where you've been waiting –

4.
How often I wait for you.
By the window. By the wall.

And how well they know you now
(the window, the wall)

by the weight of my shoulder,
gaze of my gaze.

5.
We're riding the subway after dark, and you're wearing my mother's shoes. Blue runners. The rattling train. They (the shoes) were waiting in the closet, cold under a layer of dust. You tried them all, and then we cleared it out. Shoes, dresses, everything. That night we slept hand in hand, then walked all day. Oblivious city. Only the shoe salesman, puzzled, your heel in his hand.

6.
Hanging pods and twigs:
darkened, carved there.
You kneel by the window,
waiting. In the narrow circle of a lamp.
How often by a window, or a wall.
October. Something simmers on the stove.
At last the flesh can go.
The sky yet light with a blue light.

The Four-Cornered World

I've been meaning to say something about a fellow I know. He may be old, but he doesn't look it. He's tall, broad-shouldered, a woodsman. His hair, a pure buttery white, falls past his ears as in the portraits of Handel. If you remark on it he'll modestly mention that his barber is off travelling, not a joke.

For years before I knew him, he lived in Sweden, building organs for the church. Late in life, as sometimes happens, he fell in love with a big-hearted woman who longed in turn for another life: driving a semi-trailer full of goods back and forth across the broad, rolling expanse of North America.

Now he builds violins in a woodshed, and waits for her on weekends. The forest around the house is as clean and dry and quiet as the rooms inside. He'll make you coffee, then follow cordially as you show yourself around. Spend the night, and the trolls might creep out to watch you: they're fascinated by human sleep.

My friend must be well over eighty, but he's nowhere near death. The face of the new violin is pale and smooth and lovely. If you want to know what he does for a living, he'll tell you: he works in the forest.

Our hair hangs down, and the bare withies
of the yellow willow.
Yes, we once were reptiles.

Lake in the air. Snowing. And the snowy gulls
like old bald gentlemen, walking in the park.

Much earlier in the world, monks were seen flying
to their monasteries on the high crags.
From the space shuttle, the Earth is Buddha's alms bowl.

Each flake makes a small *plash*:
the pure sound of counting.

Some mornings we have to lay ourselves
limb on limb like mating starfish,
to prolong the anguish.

It's snowing in the plum tree, adorning it
with the white jade grave bracelets
of a despised emperor of the Song Dynasty, an emperor
who longs with treelike patience to open on the world
his thousand pink eyes again. Obliging but deaf,
the scribes, wily advisors, little dark servant girls
and necromancers of the court have all been turned
to squirrels. Wars are started by whispering
and analogy, eras die with their people. Thinking of him
I drink my favourite tea, looking out on the snowy garden.

People who can foretel the future by
Communication with the spirits of the dead

HORSEMINT

Past the bicycles tied to the still-blossoming trees,
past the visiting mathematicians
conferring on the lawns in their funereal
suits, too abstracted to sit down
or move on, though the sun was nearly setting,
and one might gaze undistracted toward the lone
swimmer in the pool,
making a point about a missing theta . . .

I took
your hand and led you away,
for the thickets of mint
would be pricking up their dog-eared
leaves for the evening, among the cool
stars of daffodil
in the newly claimed shade. We picked
the tenderest, and in closets and dim rooms
our shoes and pockets would smell for days –

But mint
has another destiny: to be crushed
with sugar and bourbon
and summer ice from the bar,
where the more slovenly, shirt-sleeved,
nevertheless energetic mathematicians
might still be sitting arguing over beer, heads idly cocked
for the passage of the kitchen help . . .

Any one of them would have come with me,
yet twice I had to tug your arm,
and you were helpless as a young dog
wanting nothing more than to run with the other dogs –

and then we passed among them,
stately as gods, with our frosted drinks of wild mint,
and my slight shame. My slight shame –
and, yes, delight –
at having stolen you
out to the generous nameless meadow.

OH YES

Oh yes, I have regrets. Among the pale
escalatory criss-crossed songs of April
I have many,
not unnameable. Among them an unreasonable
regard for one or two, whom I adore as the scholar
her lost civilizations, needing
the very hairpins and winecups – to touch
whatever they touched . . .
I give it up
as I give up each breath: to take another.
Things I might have done. Of course, had I not
not done them. This headlong fall
has laws, and the first
is that we can't leave anything important
to the last, or learn what that *is*
in time to do otherwise. Other than that?
I worship the thinking hair
on the chest of a certain man. I'll dress
for no one, pay little mind
to words like "faith" and "escutcheon."
Advice I'll take from anyone, anytime.
Even these few, having come upon them:
names, dates, the young memorial grove
planted on the grounds of the university,
its green shade,
nestled at the base of thought.

A shield bearing a Coat of Arms or A ships stern bearing her Name

BED

There are whole days I would rather not leave you.
At coffee break and at lunch break and in between,
in the split-seconds between adding up figures,
for a moment I peel away the covers
and sit up, again,
to the inextinguishable day,
and your expanse gazes
up at me sadly
and the long limbs of the blankets' dishevelment
seduce me back.

There are days I would rather not leave you,
that intimate –
nothing to be said,
and no misunderstanding. Remember
the afternoon I first brought you here: the cat
jumped down in a huff
and sauntered off, showing us
his vertical tail, but you
grew wider,
and curious,
and very quiet.

There are days I would rather not so much as breathe,
but you compose my dreams,
and when they turn, when I'm at the edge
of what I can bear, I
wake suddenly –
warm sands,
and effortless wanderings of ocean music,

a sea wall where hurled bottles have
smashed at night –
held up by you.

I WAKE NOT KNOWING

I wake not knowing where I've been.
But travelling again.
To feel the animal breath inside me

for the first time, going in and out,
the corpse that will displace me
animating it.

The strangest ways of seeing
are destroyed and reinvented countless times.
Even this.

And in the morning
one who hardly knows me calls to say
she's seen me, far from here, and in a dream.

ON LEARNING THAT WANG WEI'S COUNTRY HOME IS NOW THE SITE OF A MILITARY INSTALLATION

Of your estate, they say, only a single pine remains.
I too come in summer to the mountains.
The lizards flash their blue tails and grow used to me.
At night I read history, and fall asleep.

The critics and theologians are still counting and
    arguing,
counting and arguing over and over, like old misers.
What's the point?
Even you could never choose one life over the other.
Better to drift off, imagining the past

or the future. Two boats on the dark river
that bump lightly and then pass on their way.

Blood of the earth. Lovers, hills, days,
an acre of short dark crosses
near Jenner, where the fledgling vines
sprouted one spring. Sea-wrack,
the smell of salt or guilt, fennel on the hillsides.

Rain, and rain, and rain . . .

                                        Pungent, shady,
coolest on the hottest days, then moving into sunlight
out of the deepest shade . . .

                                        Something of the harvest
too, workers bent like penitents –

But nothing of the dead, though they drink
the same rainwater, eat the same bread,
are bread.

FIRE

Even now, and in November,
where the fire passed,
and the blackening rains,
the ashes of her desire to be beautiful,
as if this were exact, a life –

as if the ashes did not lie on the ground
with the other household waste, toxic, precisely a life,
and only what escaped
had no desire to burn,
no willingness;

as if this were a life
or an entry, a record of entreaty or a door,
without forethought or desire, as in November,
irises purple in the slate rain,
the confectioner's ash and glass tears of the melted
houses,

someone's brother weeping in a hard hat,
a Centurion with a shovel,
if you want to burn a book
burn the city
(ancient saying).

And the city does burn,
chimneys pointing back at God, who else? –
endurance is not a duty,
the ashes running in the gutters,
mascara or kohl, as she turns

in the rain, away.
As if this were a life or an entry,
a record of entreaty or a door,
without forethought or desire,
as in November,

the chartreuse sourgrass flowering over the hills,
the garden that the garden has become,
the irises risen in their black beds,
a piece of old china
in the willow pattern, in the rain.

IN THE DARK

I wake and it's like a live
coal pressed between us,
though you're dreaming still, stretched across me
as if holding up the world, snoring hard
with the hard work of it,

and though it's happened before, I'm as surprised
as if the escalator had just been invented,
or the mythical pebble, unnoticed at nightfall
the first time we slept out
in a sleeping bag under the stars,

been finally found. And though you're sleeping still,
I lever you over, your chest hot and flat and dry –
and I remember again
the bad time, which we shouldn't speak of,
when you could barely move, and wouldn't eat.

You lay beside me like an open-eyed corpse,
you could see a thousand miles, but not an inch . . .
We must have gone on for a month that way,
without making a joke, and when the first bad pun
came to you I was so grateful I nearly wept.

And that night or the next, when your penis, after slow
consideration, lit up like an idea –
something in me too,
something in me that had lain too still,
long-lost in my body, lit up –

like one of those lovely living rags we find
on the beach at high tide, that knows

no loneliness but cannot move on land,
and lies there, sadly inscribing
the sand with its shape, until we touch it.

Given what love is, and how wearying it is
resisting the obvious,
that knowledge decomposes too, and as a body,

the years of useful longing
now changeless as bread, because it's Christmastime,
fairy lights in the trees,

cities seething a little in the heat-release of nightfall,
in a thousand darkened
living rooms across the continent,

what is music anyway, air spirit?
To be mineral and voluble as Mozart,
strings of lights in the shapes of fruits,

the tree among the hardened ornaments,
the castle on the packet of Dime Store nougat
making of these rooms

a continental forest
where the owl still calls,
lost kin or friendship.

Lie down in this place with the lights in the dark.
The long blue avenues have never moved.
The clockhands on the shops remind us what time is,

how its shape returns. Two figures in an upstairs window
    weeping,
and the carollers who've come from house to house
to sing below them with such tenderness.

It's late, nearly 3 A.M., but hearing her flap a cardboard box, or toss some lump of wood about, I pull the curtain back and see she's chasing the dog again – a black shape in the yard – and cackling with pleasure. She babies him. His name is Troy, although she calls him Monster.

This is our neighbour to the north. She's Greek. She told us when we first moved in. "We Greek," she said, then for a time didn't laugh at all – all in black because her mother died. We'd nod over the fence, or catch each other's eye. Having few words in common suits grief perfectly.

Our neighbours to the south are also Greek, from Crete. They brought back caper seeds this year – to plant, I guess, for memory. We know this because of the pheasant. We heard it screeching in the yard, and when we asked, he said it fell, miraculously, from the sky and into the construction yard as he was leaving work. He brought it home because he'd prayed for it. A bird to eat the seeds, then pass them through, so they could germinate.

In our little neighbourhood, as you can see, miracles still occur occasionally. It's very late, and finally the pheasant is asleep. Above the driveway, a brilliant comma moon is hanging in the sky. It looks, I think, as Galileo must have seen it.

I don't know where the others go,
those who've loved all the worlds too much
to come back to this one –
but I know where I'll come, if I can.
To these iron-quiet cypresses,
the angular blue roads and evening
sunlight off the coast. If
before I'm burned they want
my citizenship, just give them
this place, and the time.
Tell them I've fallen for one or two
merely for the beach-fire smell
of their sleeping bags, lain my head
against the collar of my own brother,
gathered the local clams
and feasted on the wild green stamens
of horsetails. Her black heart,
I quipped, running my hands
through the leaden sands that were my mother –
knowing where they go, the dead:
inconsummate, without laughter.
And yet she's here, in the continuous
wind off the headlands, in the glance
of these winding hills
as I'll be, one day, if I'm lucky,
when all of love and grief and allegiance
weigh less than a strand of hair.
Just say on my behalf "the present,"
and then look at your shoes. I'll be
among the female horsetails,
frowzy and Medusal in a roadside ditch,

waiting for the male, and spring.
Look for me.

WINTER FALLOW

Ice in the trees and mist on the land.
The furrows fall straight, ribboning the field.
The furrows are snow, the fields are snow.
The news piles up. The trees are in their chrysalis.
This too is a song,
                    and this.

VESPERS, FIRENZE

There is no world without art,
and the sound of art is blue, *triste*,
the sadness around the eyes
while the gut smiles. *What is death?*
or *When is the body purified?*
A playful absence – the last ten minutes
stinking in the rain. When meticulous love
is gone, but made things remain.

READING LORCA

The will in me, like my breasts,
hadn't yet begun to grow.
But that blue diaphanous
sky with its core of iron
drew me. To the window.
A filigree of trees.
Twilight, owls. Moons, lamps.
The one who listened
is the one who always listens.
I rested the heavy book against my belly
and my mother said to do my homework.
I was young. I had all these words.
All these words,
and few rules,
save one.

HELLO DESIRE

Hello desire, you've been gone awhile.
In whose arms have you been sleeping?
As fragrance is remembrance, love
work, and a rose the horticulturist's: *Bonfire Night*
or *Burning Cloud*, *Attraction* and other hybrids –
now that I'm halfway to being old,
wanting only to be born. *Die Welt*
– the world, that is – from an unknown seedling,
cross *Peer Gynt.* Nodes of irony, longing, bitter charm.
Desire. If I were young I'd have only to name you.
Blue Moon at twilight. *Handsome Friend.*
Loose your petals.
Think on me.

The italicized line in "Waking the Ghost of Du Fu" is a quotation from "Fleeing Through Pengya" by Du Fu, as translated by Yang Xianyi and Gladys Yang in their book *Poetry and Prose of the Tang and Song*, published in Beijing in 1984 by Panda Books.

The section titles are borrowed from *Introduction to the Introduction to Wang Wei* by Pain Not Bread. Thanks to the members of Pain Not Bread.

"To the Grey Squirrel" is for Bob Amussen.
"In the Forest" is for Oskar and Gunvor Sundstrom.

Special thanks to Kim Maltman – this collection owes much to the synergistic effects of collaborative editing. Thanks also to Stan Dragland for his quick eye, and to Jan Zwicky and Don McKay for listening. Thanks to Sue Schenck for the author photo and to Jamelie Hassan for the cover image.

The Canada Council and the Ontario Arts Council are gratefully acknowledged for their support, as are those journals in which the poems first appeared: *Arc*, *Exile*, *The Fiddlehead*, *Hence*, *Hubbub*, *The Malahat Review*, *Nimrod*, *Orbis*, *Poetry Canada Review*, *PRISM International*, *Quarry*, *Saturday Night*; "Moon Tub," "Hello Desire," and "You Leave the City . . ." first appeared in *Prairie Schooner*; "Life Among Flowers" and "From the Night Interstate" appeared in *The Southern Review*; "It's Raining" and "Starting the Tape" appeared in the anthology *Sudden Miracles*, Eight Women Poets, edited by Rhea Tregebov; "Late Luncheon" was first published, along with the poems

"The Technology of Cruelty," "Recipe for Divertimento in D, K.136," and "Practicing Bach," by Kim Maltman, Don McKay, and Jan Zwicky as Kitchen Table Broadsides No. 1.